Corstop
An Edwardian
Excavation

Photographs from the 1906–14 excavations of the
Roman Site at Corbridge, Northumberland

by M C Bishop

A field camera being used to record an altar to Jupiter Dolichenus and Caelestis Brigantia (RIB 1131) soon after it has been excavated. One of the supervisory staff (left, wearing a boater) has been joined by two visitors for this informal portrait group, presumably taken by J P Gibson in 1910 (Corbridge Excavation Fund)

Contents

Foreword

Corbridge, even more than most Roman sites, appears as it is because of the activities of archaeologists. This booklet is an insight into the process of excavation over eighty years ago, and sheds a fascinating light on why 'Corstopitum' looks as it does.

Christopher Young, Regional Director, English Heritage Historic Properties North

Preface and Acknowledgements

The photographs in this volume are drawn from a number of sources, although all ultimately derive from the official photographs taken during the *Corstopitum* excavations, mostly by J P Gibson (1906–12). Apart from prints belonging to the Trustees of the Corbridge Excavation Fund, now in the collections of Corbridge Roman Site Museum and the English Heritage Historic Plans room at Keysign House, these consist of copies of prints held by the Society of Antiquaries of Newcastle upon Tyne and the Northumberland Record Office (NRO), and glass negatives likewise held by the NRO.

The decision to mount a small exhibition of some of the more striking of these photographs naturally led to thoughts of a modest publication that would both serve the needs of visitors to the exhibition, wishing to know more about what they had seen, and specialists, many of whom will be unaware of the richness of the collection and some of the surprises it holds.

Many individuals and organisations have helped in the preparation of both the exhibition and this book and it is only fitting that they should be recorded here. Martha Andrews 'brainstormed' when required, read draft copies of the text, and helped in numerous ways; Mrs Sally Bird, Northumberland County Council, facilitated access to the Gibson material in the NRO, and Mr J Gibson kindly allowed its reproduction. Charles Daniels, Chair of the Trustees of the Corbridge Excavation Fund, likewise agreed to the use of material belonging to the Fund. Mrs D Fairless and Mrs M Witton generously permitted the reproduction of photographs in their possession. Philip Freeman advised on the background to Haverfield's and his students' involvement in the excavations. Thanks are also due to Sandra Green, Curator of English Heritage's Historic Plans Room. Other help during the preparation of the exhibition was rendered by Christies of South Kensington; Beryl Clayton-Hibbott, Ashbourne House Antiques, Hexham; Alec Coles, Hancock Museum, Tyne & Wear Museums Service; and Mr Robin Tuppen of Thomas Smith Trug Shop, Herstmonceux. The driving force behind both the exhibition and this book was Georgina Plowright, curator of the Hadrian's Wall Museums for English Heritage, inspired by a suggestion from Alison Bramley. The prints for both the exhibition and this volume were expertly prepared by Neil Askew. Publication was made possible with the aid of a grant from Northumberland County Council.

Introduction

Roman Corbridge

The modern visitor to the Roman remains at Corbridge sees only a tiny portion of what was once a large, sprawling, frontier town (Fig 1). Since it was given to the nation in the 1930s, archaeological work has concentrated within this area, now in the care of English Heritage, but earlier excavations had already shown the extent and richness of the remains of the town. The photographs in this small book not only show how those excavations were undertaken, but also give some idea of what still lies beneath the fields around the monument as it is today. The scale of the project was impressive, for it was an exercise in clearing a large area, as earlier excavations on the Roman towns of Silchester (near Reading) and Caerwent (near Newport in Gwent) had been at the end of the nineteenth century.

The *Corstopitum* Excavations

At the beginning of the twentieth century, Francis Haverfield, Camden Professor of Ancient History at the University of Oxford, was one of the leading figures in the study of Roman Britain. He began his career as a schoolmaster at Lancing College in Sussex. Whilst there, he taught himself the study of Latin inscriptions and became so proficient that he was invited to contribute to the supplementary British volume of the *Ephemeris Epigraphica*, an important collection of newly discovered Latin inscriptions. Not content with that, he then began to acquaint himself with the Roman remains of Britain and Europe. He was a member of countless archaeological societies and sat on numerous committees: one such was the Northumberland County History Committee.

It was at Haverfield's instigation that the Northumberland County History Committee decided that archaeological excavation was desirable on the Roman site just west of Corbridge, widely known as *Corstopitum* (even before excavation had begun, the surviving form of the Roman name was not generally believed; documents recently found at *Vindolanda*, just a few miles to the west, suggest that the Roman name might have been *Coria*). This Committee was responsible for preparing the volume on the history of the parish of Corbridge and wished to assess the quality of the remains of the Roman site. They were fortunate in gaining the enthusiasm and support of the landowner, Captain J H Cuthbert of Beaufront Castle. After an initial season, it was clear that the site 'possesses unusual interest' (Forster 1908, 205); the Corbridge Excavation Committee was formed in 1907 and, every summer until 1914, a team of archaeologists – both specialists and labourers – descended on the site and proceeded to uncover one of the most fascinating sites of the Roman north-west frontier. Haverfield remained the mastermind behind the project, supplying young scholars from Oxford as excavation staff, visiting regularly whilst work was in progress, and writing contributions for the annual interim reports published in *Archaeologia Aeliana* from 1907–15, as well as statements on their progress in the *Proceedings* of the Society of Antiquaries of London.

That first season of excavations in 1906 was supervised by Leonard Woolley (Fig 2), who was soon to become famous for his archaeological work in the Near East. Woolley was suggested to Haverfield by Arthur Evans, excavator of the Minoan palace of Knossos on Crete, but in his memoirs, published in 1953, Woolley was rather scathing about

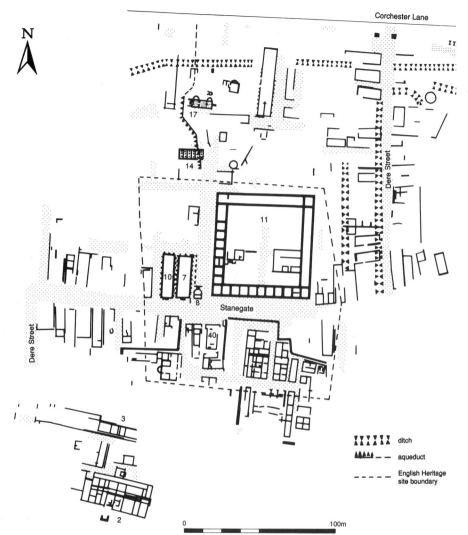

Fig 1 Plan showing the extent of the 1906–14 excavations (after Bishop and Dore 1989)

those early experiences at Corbridge (*see below, p 10*). He was assisted by R H Forster and W H Knowles and they took over the supervision of the *Corstopitum* excavations in 1907 when Woolley left to dig in the East. Forster was to supervise work and Knowles, a trained architect, was in charge of planning the site. To assist them, Haverfield sent some of his best students from Oxford. These, who were to include R L Atkinson, J P Bushe-Fox, G L Cheesman, and P Newbold, started with charge of an area of the excavation and later progressed onto excavating their own sites (Atkinson and Bushe-Fox began work at Wroxeter in 1912 and Bushe-Fox subsequently became Chief Inspector of

Fig 2 Leonard Woolley (left) and J P Gibson (right) (Mrs M Witton & The Trustees of the Clayton Collection)

Ancient Monuments). In addition, they had the services of arguably the leading archaeological photographer in the region, to help them record the project.

The Photographs

Like excavation itself, the practice of archaeological photography has changed somewhat since those early days. Nowadays archaeologists view it as another form of record of the excavated site and usually prepare sites carefully before a photograph is taken. A scale of a known size is included and, more often than not, some indication of the direction of north, and perhaps even the number of the feature being studied. Most importantly, the area to be photographed is cleared of all extraneous equipment and archaeologists. If members of the excavation staff are to be in the picture, it is as 'human scales' or used to mark specific features (such as a line of large postholes). Occasionally, informal 'human interest' shots showing the archaeologists at work will be taken, perhaps for publicity purposes, but a very clear distinction exists between the two types of photograph.

The photographic record of the *Corstopitum* excavations was initially in the hands of J P Gibson (Fig 2), a local amateur archaeologist and photographer (although a pharmacist by profession, with a shop in Hexham). Gibson used his photographs to make postcards (*see Fig 37*) which were then sold to visitors, providing a useful source of revenue when funds were low for the excavation. The workmen had to be paid, and although the various committees provided funding, it was nevertheless essential to charge an extrance fee for visitors and sell postcards to help defray expenses. Gibson died in 1912 and Forster took over the photography.

One of the things that makes the photographs of the 1906–14 *Corstopitum* project so

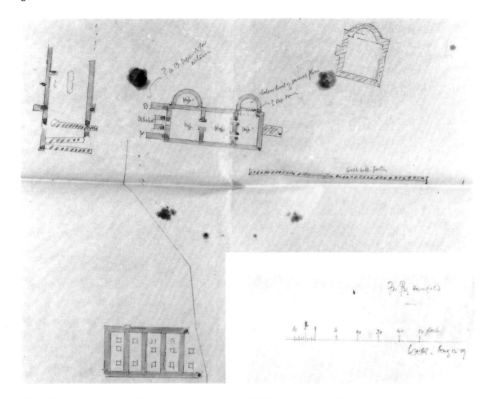

Fig 3 Detail from a pencil and wash plan by W H Knowles of the Site 17 bath-house, with (inset) his initials and the date Aug 12 '09 (1909; Corbridge Excavation Fund)

interesting is that they are a record of the progress of the excavations and, whilst they include views that have largely been cleared of excavation personnel, sufficient of them show the men at work to be a useful social document on the methods of archaeologists in Edwardian England. They are also, almost without exception, cluttered with the tools and equipment used: small piles of finds can be seen in nearly all of them.

However, the photographs serve a more important purpose beyond mere curiosity value. Indeed, they present us with many details which cannot now be retrieved by any other means. For example, after part of the site had been given to the nation, the buildings of the central area were consolidated in the 1930s and '40s. This process seems to have involved 'tidying up' some parts, perhaps even removing archaeologically significant aspects of a building. Here, the photographs hint at just how much we have lost and provide some missing detail.

The Importance of the *Corstopitum* Project

The *Corstopitum* excavations, although cut short by the outbreak of the Great War, were certainly significant in the history of the study of Roman Britain. They were contemporary with James Curle's important (and, for its time, very advanced) work at the Roman fort of *Trimontium* at Newstead, near Melrose in Scotland, and there seems to have been a frequent exchange of information between the archaeologists at Corbridge and Newstead. Moreover, the *Corstopitum* project served to train a new generation of scholars who went on to become great names in British archaeology. In this it had fulfilled one of Haverfield's wishes, although apparently not one with which he had begun the project. It is perhaps no coincidence that, 50 years later, training excavations run by the Universities of Durham and Newcastle upon Tyne were to provide many of the leading names in present-day archaeology.

The Excavators

The Supervisors

Leonard Woolley was working as Assistant Keeper in the Ashmolean Museum in Oxford when he was asked to participate in the *Corstopitum* project. His later unease at his own participation is interesting:

> In point of fact I had never so much as seen an excavation, I had never studied archaeological methods even from books (there were none at the time dealing with the subject), and I had not any idea of how to make a survey or a groundplan; apart from being used to handling antiquities in a museum, and that only for a few months, I had no qualifications at all. (Woolley 1953, 14–15)

The shock of being thrown in at the deep end had evidently lasted more than four decades, although it is not apparent in Maria Hoyer's account of her meeting with him (*see below, pp 45–8*). Ultimately, his criticisms of Haverfield's overall supervision of the excavations probably say more about the maturer Woolley's methods as an archaeologist than those of Haverfield:

> I was very anxious to learn, and it was a disappointment to me that Haverfield only looked in at the excavation one day in the week and then was concerned only to know what had been found – I don't think that he ever criticized or corrected anything. (*ibid*)

Robert Forster was a native of Corbridge, the son of a mining engineer. He was also a barrister, novelist, poet, archaeologist, and Captain of the Thames Rowing Club. In 1899 he published a collection of essays with an archaeological theme, *The Amateur Antiquary*, which included an imaginative description of Corbridge in Roman times:

> Corstopitum is a curious, irregular little place. The cramped fortress, which Julius Agricola planted here on the ruins of some old Otadene stronghold, has already been swallowed by the thriving town, to which peace and commerce have given birth. There is no troop in garrison now, but some two thousand rough, pleasure-loving soldiers are quartered within a few miles of the place, and Corstopitum lives on them. Even at this late hour the forum is ringing with the clamour of bargainers; for during the afternoon various parties have come hither on leave from Cilurnum, Hunnum, and Vindobala; and every man of them is bent on enjoyment. Garrison life in these Wall-fortresses is a monotonous form of existence; and many a rough soldier knows no other charm to beguile its dulness, than the memory or expectation of these '*noctes Corstopitanae*'.

Little could he know that, only seven years later, he was to be excavating on that very site and, upon the departure of Woolley for the Near East, take charge of the day-to-day running of the dig.

Unlike Woolley, Forster was already a respected archaeologist who had papers on

Fig 4 Forster is seen here, outside the site museum, wearing a boater, characteristic of the supervisors on the site. Note the trug full of finds near his feet (Corbridge Excavation Fund)

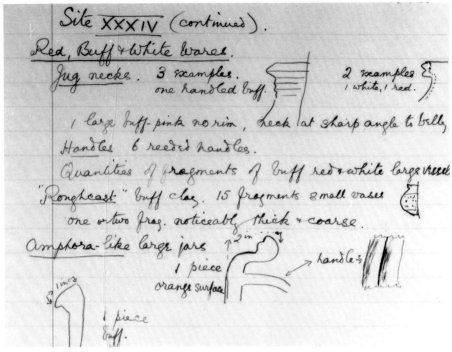

Fig 5 Part of one of the site notebooks recording pieces of pottery recovered from Site 34 in 1911. The hand is that of Newbold (Corbridge Excavation Fund)

Hadrian's Wall published when he came to work at Corbridge. He lived in Putney and travelled up each year, staying in Corbridge for the duration of the excavation. Surviving letters of his to Haverfield, dating to the 1913 and 1914 seasons, show that his wife came up too (they married in 1913) and that she managed to find the time for reconstructing pottery from the excavations, as well as some dressmaking. In both of those years, the Forsters stayed in Kingsley House in Corchester Terrace, overlooking the excavations. His colleague Henry Knowles later recalled that he was well-liked by the labourers on the site.

Henry Knowles was an architect by training (responsible for Kings College, now part of the University of Newcastle upon Tyne) but possessed an active interest in, and no little aptitude for, archaeology. He was involved in the excavation of parts of the castle in Newcastle upon Tyne.

Other Supervisory and Specialist Staff Involved

The list of archaeologists working on the *Corstopitum* project included those who were to go on to be famous, as well as those who have vanished without trace. These included R L Atkinson (pottery); J P Bushe-Fox (pottery), later the Chief Inspector of Ancient

Fig 6 Typical labourers on the Corstopitum excavations (Corbridge Excavation Fund)

Monuments for the Ministry of Works; G L Cheesman (pottery), who wrote a seminal book on the auxiliary soldiers of the Roman army, before being killed in the Great War; J G N Clift (excavation and planning); H H E Craster (coins); C Dodd; R H Forster (excavation & photography); J P Gibson (photography); Prof F Haverfield (inscriptions); R C Hedley; G F Hill; W H Knowles (surveying & planning); Prof Lebour; W B Liebert; Prof Meek (animal bone); P Newbould (pottery); D S Robertson; F G Simpson (excavation), who was to be one of the great names in Hadrian's Wall studies; W H St John Hope (planning); Mill Stephenson (planning); G H Stevenson; N Whatley (pottery); C L Woolley (excavation), another 'great' in the archaeological firmament.

Most of those noted as specializing in pottery were apparently also acting as excavation supervisors.

The Labourers

The hard work of excavation, shifting tons of soil to uncover the remains, was accomplished by labourers from the area around Corbridge and Hexham. These men had no training in archaeology and it was the job of the supervisors to ensure that they knew what to do and how to do it. The photographs show them wearing cloth caps (and the occasional bowler), heavy boots, and invariably working with the pick and shovel. The size of the labour force varied from year to year: there were between six and nine men in 1906, but a group photo of 1908 shows 25 men and one lad. By 1914, the number was down to a maximum of 16. Unlike a modern excavation, it was common to use local labour, rather than specialists brought in from outside. Hence many people now living in the Corbridge and Hexham area have relatives who participated in the *Corstopitum* excavations.

Fig 7 Moving the spoil (1910; Corbridge Excavation Fund)

Fig 8 Archaeology can be thirsty work in summer. The young trug-carrier provides refreshment for colleagues in the area to the east of the remains visible today (1910; Society of Antiquaries of Newcastle upon Tyne)

The Excavations

By 1910, *Corstopitum* had become one of the first training excavations in the history of British archaeology. Haverfield wrote:

> We can include in our staff a few beginners in archaeology, and put them in the way of learning how to conduct excavations, how to handle workmen, and how to deal with and record finds. This practical training of future archaeologists is a new effort, never yet attempted in any English excavations, and we hope that, as we succeed in developing it and learning how to do it better, we may prove to have done something towards the uncovering of Wroxeter and other Roman sites awaiting the spade. (Haverfield 1911, 478–9)

Each season consisted of up to four months' work (July–October). The Oxford students had charge of a number of workmen who worked in a rather different way to modern archaeologists. The line of diligent trowellers so familiar from present-day excavations was not in use then, most spoil being shifted with the aid of pick, shovel, and long-handled broom, with a crowbar to move particularly large stones. Soil was removed by wheelbarrow and a small side-tipping rail cart. The edges of the trenches, or sections, were kept very straight and clean and consequently the photographs are quite informative for the modern archaeologist with a hand-lens. Although their comprehension of archaeological processes was less refined than it is today, the basic principles of stratification were both understood and observed, a fact that is evident from the published accounts (and most especially in George MacDonald's discussion of the circumstances of the find of gold coins in 1911: see MacDonald 1912). It is often said that archaeologists at this time could not distinguish structures made of wood and merely sought stone buildings, but the Corbridge excavators certainly recorded wooden features when they occurred.

At first, the nature of the site presented its own problems too, for the 1906 and 1907 seasons concentrated on the area of the scarp between the river and the plateau above it:

> The trenches, especially those on the slope and at the bridge road, were on the average considerably deeper than those at Silchester, and the débris to be moved was full of massive blocks and more difficult to handle than the débris usually found on sites, such as Silchester, lying outside a stone country. In working on a heavy slope, the greatest difficulty is the disposal of the excavated earth, so that it may be replaced without waste of labour. (Forster 1908, 207–8)

Few documents survive from the 1906–14 excavations, but there are some notebooks and at least one plan. We can see that the pottery found, worked on by Cheesman, Newbold, Bushe-Fox, and Atkinson, was logged in notebooks with sketch sections of the various vessel types (Fig 5). The surviving plan – of a bath-house, Site 17, excavated in 1909 – shows Knowles' method of drawing up his surveys (Fig 3). Executed in pencil and grey wash, it was a field sketch for Prof Haverfield.

Fig 9 Site 7, the fountain. When first found in 1907, it was thought to be a temple of some sort but its true nature was rapidly realised. This view is particularly interesting because some of the principle tools of the early excavators – pick, shovel, crow bar, and scrubbing brush – have been quite consciously left within view, perhaps as an indication of scale. The technique of excavation seems to have involved removing the overburden with pick and shovel, then brushing stone walls clean with a long-handled broom. Finer excavation tools, such as trowels, are seldom evident in any of the pictures (1907; NRO 1876/F/1885)

Fig 10 Vast amounts of topsoil had to be removed during the course of the excavations, and much of it put back again when a campaign was finished. The tipper waggon in this photograph (see also Fig 7), freewheeling with two passengers, was used to move this spoil from the trenches to the spoilheaps. The tracks upon which the cart ran can often be seen at the edges of trenches. There was even a small turntable enabling several different trenches to be served by the one system (1910; Society of Antiquaries of Newcastle upon Tyne)

Fig 11 Top: this is the rear range of rooms from the headquarters building of the early forts, in the course of excavation. This building is still visible in the western half of the courtyard of Site 11 and even the edges of the original trenches are still discernible (1908; NRO 1876/F/1921)
Bottom: A detail of the inside of the wall of the shrine (or aedes*) of the headquarters building. It shows the voids that are all that remain of the timber uprights of an earlier phase that have been incorporated within a later stone structure. This inside wall was plastered (traces are evident in this photograph) and painted yellow (1908; NRO 1876/F/1922)*

Fig 12 The headquarters building in Site 11 two years after it had been excavated. The trench had been left open and is now overgrown and the edges crumbling (they have been reinforced in places by drystone walling, formed from the large amounts of rubble the excavators found on the site) (1910; Corbridge Excavation Fund)

*Fig 13 Robert Forster (in boater) overseeing the excavations of the portico area, in front of the two granaries (Sites 8 and 10). Successive resurfacings of the Stanegate, the road running in front of the buildings, meant that it was considerably higher than their lowest courses (note the roadside drain half way up the columns of the portico). It has been suggested that pictures like this illustrate the early excavators' tendency to destroy important archaeological layers in their search for the plans of buildings, but careful reading of the published reports suggests that this judgement is a little too harsh, although techniques were primitive by comparison with those now in use. 1909. (**Corbridge Excavation Fund**)*

Fig 14 Workmen clearing the commanding officer's house belonging to the early fort. Like the fort headquarters building, with which it was contemporary, it survived the demolition of the fort in the mid second century AD. Note that one pickman is working with two shovellers, an indication of the amount of material that these men were capable of moving. The trench sides are always impressively straight and vertical and have the appearance of having been finished with a pick. Note how close the spoil is piled to the edge of the trench; nowadays a considerable distance would be left for reasons of safety and access (1910; Society of Antiquaries of Newcastle upon Tyne)

Fig 15 Excavations to the east of the site now in the care of English Heritage. Again two shovellers work with one pickman. The wheelbarrow and planks are used to remove spoil in exactly the same fashion as on a modern archaeological site. Note the large amount of rubble on the sides of the trenches, some of it used to revet the spoilheaps (1910; Society of Antiquaries of Newcastle upon Tyne)

Fig 16 A modest attempt at reconstruction archaeology. A collapsed arch was found in the south range of Site 11 (top) and its constituent blocks (voussoirs) were numbered in situ (with painted dots) and the whole thing temporarily re-erected (bottom). The ultimate fate of the arch is now unknown. The voussoirs are noteworthy in that they are from a barrel vaulted ceiling of a kind also found in the bath-house at Chesters (1909; Corbridge Excavation Fund)

Roman Corbridge Revealed

Photographs of excavated buildings can often reveal more than just plans or descriptions, and they are invaluable to later researchers who did not witness the actual excavation. Some say that archaeology is not a science because it is an unrepeatable experiment – the very process of excavation destroys many of the more subtle clues to what has happened, usually leaving only the more durable (eg stone walls) for display purposes.

Fig 17 An unrepeatable experiment. The west range of Site 11 as it first appeared when excavated. Note how the trench follows the wall. Such 'wall-chasing' is deplored by modern archaeologists, but was generally thought acceptable at the time (1908; Corbridge Excavation Fund)

Fig 18 Consolidation work in the 1930s means that much of the north-east corner of Site 11, the large courtyard building, looks very different now to when it was first excavated. At the time of its uncovering, it was noted that the foundations appeared to have been deliberately toppled and this is dramatically illustrated in this photograph. The building was abandoned before it was completed, probably in the second half of the second century AD (1910; Corbridge Excavation Fund)

Fig 19 The west granary (Site 10) has an inspection hatch at its south end, enabling the ventilated area beneath the floor to be examined. This doorway had a timber frame and door. However, this was blocked up with a stone wall for some reason, but the Roman who did this only took the door off its hinges and then built the wall within the timber frame, with the result that although the timber had rotted away, its outline could still be seen when excavated. This demonstrates just how valuable a record these photographs can be, since no trace of the blocking wall now survives and no detailed drawing seems to have been made (1908; Corbridge Excavation Fund)

Fig 20 Styles of consolidation change with time and although it is no longer apparent, when the east granary (Site 8) was first excavated, the mortar and the rubble cores of the walls preserved the outline impressions of the facing stones which had long since been robbed away by later inhabitants of the region, eager for ready-dressed stone. These impressions were probably removed during the 1930s consolidation programme (1908; Corbridge Excavation Fund)

Fig 21 Top: the east and west granaries were first uncovered in 1908, but the landowner gave permission for them to be left open for visitors in subsequent years of the project to be able to see them. 1909. Bottom: in 1910 the east granary was cleaned up and partially consolidated, evidently with a mortar capping (to prevent weather damage to the vulnerable cores of the walls). Its western neighbour received similar treatment in 1911 (1910; Corbridge Excavation Fund)

Fig 22 One of the accusations laid against excavators of the late nineteenth and early twentieth centuries is their inability to recognize the remains of timber features. This was certainly not true of the archaeologists at Corbridge, although their task was made dramatically easier when timber posts rotted in situ to leave voids, as in this instance, in front of the fountain (Site 7). This, one of three timber post-holes, may have belonged to one of the granaries of the early fort that lies beneath the area in care (1909; Corbridge Excavation Fund)

Fig 23 To the north of the area now in care were a number of interesting structures. Shown here is Site 14, a rectangular store building with a floor raised on stone pillars to aid ventilation. Many of the Corstopitum excavation photographs show small piles of finds or bones, evidently waiting to be placed in a trug. Note the small heap of pottery sherds in the foreground: even now, archaeologists are prone to make small piles in this way if they lack a finds tray! On the edge of the trench is a signpost: these were apparently put up all over the excavation for the benefit of visitors (1909; Corbridge Excavation Fund)

Fig 24 Another site to the north is a small bath-house, Site 17. This also has its floor raised on stone pillars, but here to permit heated air to circulate underneath (a hypocaust), there were three main rooms with two apsidal plunge baths on the north side. This view shows Corchester Towers in the background, a school at the time of the excavations (1909; Corbridge Excavation Fund)

Fig 25 The early excavations exposed the remains of a late building above the east range and a note on a print of this photograph confirms that it shows the wall of that building in section. It is much more crudely fashioned than earlier Roman work. Only the south range of Site 11 was ever completed and the east and west ranges seem to have fallen out of use and been covered in the later Roman period (1910; Corbridge Excavation Fund)

Fig 26 The fountain (see Fig 9) was fed by an aqueduct drawing water from the Cor Burn and part of the stone channel for this was thought to have been found to the north of the area presently in care. A remarkable feature here is the shallowness of the topsoil, compared to the deep sections all around Site 11 not far to the south (compare Fig 27). In fact, the Roman land surface rose from the edge of the scarp overlooking the Tyne to where Corchester Lane now runs. Modern agricultural activity has tended to level out this area since the eighteenth century, when the ruins of Roman Corbridge were largely flattened (1909; Corbridge Excavation Fund)

Fig 27 Site 11 under excavation (compare Fig 17), with the trench broadened to cover the whole width of the west range. The men working in the background help to give some idea of the depth of soil between the modern and Roman ground surface levels (1908; Corbridge Excavation Fund)

Bits and Pieces

The excavators not only photographed the buildings and each other, but also the more portable items they discovered. Sculpture, architectural fragments, metal and wooden objects, and even pottery. These photographs can be useful to the modern archaeologist in a number of ways. First they can show us things that are now missing. Second they can help us work out where things come from if we do not already know.

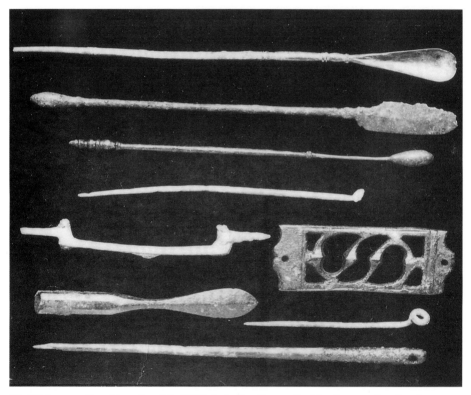

Fig 28 Copper alloy objects found in 1910, including five medical implements (top four items, and left-hand object in the sixth row). This photograph not only helps date the discovery of these unusual items and provide an approximate provenance for them (since we know which parts of Corbridge were being dug in that year), it also shows two which are now missing. Other objects include part of a sword scabbard and a belt plate (fifth row), a pin (right-hand side, sixth row), and a needle (bottom row) (1910; Corbridge Excavation Fund)

Fig 29 The early excavation photographs can be invaluable in identifying objects which have now disappeared (some objects were given to workers on the site as souvenirs, a practice no longer encouraged in archaeology). This is a stamped tile of the legio IX Hispana and this picture is the only record of its having been found at Corbridge. The number '40' was painted on by the excavators (probably in 1912) to indicate that it came from Site 40. This particular tile stamp, a known type of the ninth legion, may seem unusual in giving the Roman numeral for 9 as 'VIIII' instead of 'IX'. However, this was quite a common practice in Roman times, particularly in the first century AD. Parallel examples of this die stamp have been found at Carlisle and Scalesceugh, thought to be a legionary works depot near Carlisle, and are thought to date to the latter part of the first century AD (1912?; Corbridge Excavation Fund)

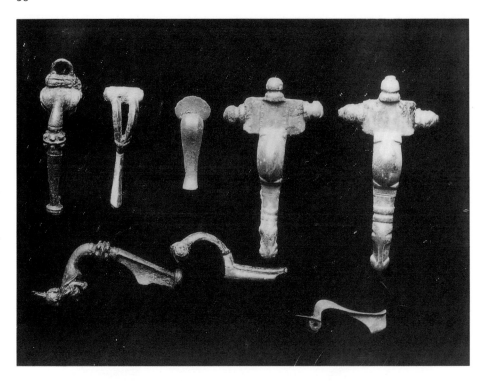

Fig 30 Surprising finds during the excavation of Site 11 were two cruciform Saxon brooches (top row, right) and an associated set of glass beads (not shown here). The brooches, now missing and only published as drawings, are characteristic of the sixth century AD, and thus probably belong to the earliest Saxon presence in this area. It has been suggested that there may have been a Saxon burial ground in the ruins of Corbridge. The Saxons later used stone from the Roman town to build their settlement (and most notably St Andrew's church) on the site of modern Corbridge (1908; Corbridge Excavation Fund)

Fig 31 The excavations in the west range of Site 11 uncovered a number of iron tools, which it was thought might have been abandoned in a hurry during an enemy attack (although such explanations nowadays seem a little fanciful). Many other iron finds came to light during the nine campaigns of excavation. A photograph such as this can be very helpful in identifying unmarked objects in the museum collection (1910; Corbridge Excavation Fund)

Fig 32 Roman Corbridge has produced large amounts of stone, both rubble and dressed stone, as well as many examples of sculptural and architectural material. Much of this had been re-used by the Romans as building material. Seen here is a general pile of sculptural odds and ends (1910; Society of Antiquaries of Newcastle upon Tyne)

Fig 33 Lifting the inscription to the Eastern sun god Sol Invictus (RIB 1137) found in one of the layers beneath the latest surface of the Stanegate, this inscription is shown being lifted (top left), carried over to the site museum (top right), and erected for a record photograph (bottom left). Record shots like this (bottom right) were of such high quality that they were used in the interim report publication (1911; Corbridge Excavation Fund)

Fig 34 Shown here is a stone pillar which is now missing, showing a crudely incised figure of a man. Once again, a record photograph proves invaluable to later generations in the absence of the real thing (1908; Society of Antiquaries of Newcastle upon Tyne)

Fig 35 A detail of the figure shown in Fig 34 (1908; Society of Antiquaries of Newcastle upon Tyne)

Fig 36 From fairly early on in the excavations, it was realised that so much material was being found that somewhere was needed to display it for visitors to the site. One of the excavation huts was duly adapted for the purpose. Both exterior (top) and interior (bottom) views are seen here (1910 or later; Corbridge Excavation Fund)

A Visit to the Corstopitum Excavations

In 1907, a visitor to the excavations, Maria A Hoyer, recorded her impressions in writing and later published them as part of an account of a walk along Hadrian's Wall, *By the Roman Wall. Notes on a Summer Holiday*, published a year later. The following extract from that book recounts the visit, whilst the photographs, here matched with the text for the first time, illustrate some of the things she saw. The young man she mentions is almost certainly Leonard Woolley, who supervised that year's campaign until his departure for Egypt in October.

After inspecting the church we inquired our way to the excavations, and we were directed to go down the hill and along by the river, which we did, following a narrow, straight, sunk road on its margin. This road we were afterwards told was the mediaeval road to Carlisle. On one side a bank of rough grass and low growth of willows lay between us and the fast flowing stream, with a sloping, hilly field on our right. Presently, the road leading through a copse, we saw on the right hand a steep bank, up which there was a rough attempt at steps, while a notice-board informed all whom it might concern that non-subscribers could see the excavations on payment of sixpence.

We mounted the steps and found ourselves in a cornfield, which rose somewhat steeply and where men were at work digging trenches recklessly amid the yellowing grain. The ground was further ornamented with little flags of

Fig 37 The Corbridge Lion, shown here soon after its discovery. It is displayed with two matching coping stones, all probably from a funerary monument originally (although the Lion was re-used as a fountain). This is one of Gibson's first Corstopitum postcards (1907; Mrs M Witton).

Fig 38 The 'Tower' mentioned by the young man was a rectangular extension to the terrace on Site 2 (the corridor house). By the time the interim report was published in 1908, the excavators no longer thought it to be a tower, calling it instead a 'bellavista'. (1907; NRO 1876/F/1876)

different colours on short sticks stuck about the field. We began to peer about and make our way from one little digging to another, when we observed a young man issue from a little wooden hut at the top of the field and go across to inspect some of the men's work. 'That is the Boss,' we exclaimed. 'Let us go and talk to him!' We made our way towards the gentleman, and he turned to us, seeing, no doubt, expectation in our eye. Almost the first word he said was, 'Have you seen the Tower?'

We gasped a little and gazed round.

We certainly did not see any building of that description, and answered meekly that we had seen nothing except a reference to sixpences, which we there and then proffered. Communications having been thus opened he took us to see the Tower. As its walls did not arise above the surface of the ground we felt with some relief that we had not been so unobservant as his words seemed to imply.

We found our cicerone a most interesting guide. The lowest part of the excavation, he said, had revealed a large house. He first explained that Corstopitum was not a military Station but a Roman civilian town. It was situated on Watling Street, which just below had crossed the Tyne: some of his men were then at work digging where he believed they would find the foundations of the Bridge. The tower of which he had spoken, and of which he had found the foundations, was connected with a large house which was not of the Pompeian

Fig 39 Left: hypocaust (under-floor heating) in a corridor of Site 2, the corridor house. The small flags were probably used for surveying (1907; NRO 1876/F/1883). Right: a trench placed with the intention of uncovering the north abutment of the Roman bridge over the river. Unfortunately nothing conclusive was found, even though the south abutment and the bases of several Roman piers were still visible in the river then, as they are now (1907; Society of Antiquaries of Newcastle upon Tyne)

form, but of what he called the corridor type, which was almost peculiar to England. He had come on this house almost by chance while digging a deep trench to find the different levels. He had easily found the Roman level, and had dug through to the neolithic level, where he had discovered flint instruments. He wanted to see if there had not been a British camp or settlement here before the Romans came.

He further explained that the town had been built in terraces rising one above another, but that the land had been so deeply ploughed that the edges of the terraces were sloped away. The lowest part he had explored was the large house before mentioned consisting of several large rooms. He had unearthed some interesting hypocausts, tall and slender ones, which he said was an early type. Above this he had come on two terraced walls, along one of which were a number of stones with square sockets cut in them. He thought they had been used for wooden posts to support a penthouse roof along the terrace wall. In the big house they had found a large ornamental cistern, and then he took us up to his wooden hut to show us a piece of sculpture which they had come upon only the week before. It was a lion crouching on the back of a stag, at whose throat he was

Fig 40 The corridor on Site 3, with the socket stones thought to support timber uprights for a roof (1907; Society of Antiquaries of Newcastle upon Tyne)

tearing. There was a hole for water to pass through, and it had been part of the adornment of the cistern.

They had found no altars, but about thirty coins; a silver one of Domitian he showed us; it was black, and he said the silver turned black, the copper green. He had got a good many pieces of the beautiful red Samian ware, one fine bowl he was joining together. It had the potters mark on it, by which they knew where it was made. The beautiful glaze of the Samian is a lost art; analysis, he said, gave no result. He also showed us a beautiful flint arrowhead which he had found, and a stylus, and best of all, the first object he had dug up was a ring bearing the word Success!

We did envy that young man his post and his work. Then we parted, wishing him good luck with his digging. The ring seemed a good omen. After this we went back to the town intent on getting luncheon.

From: Maria A Hoyer, *By the Roman Wall. Notes on a Summer Holiday* (London 1908)